Steam South & West

Michael Messenger

TWELVEHEADS PRESS

TRURO   2019

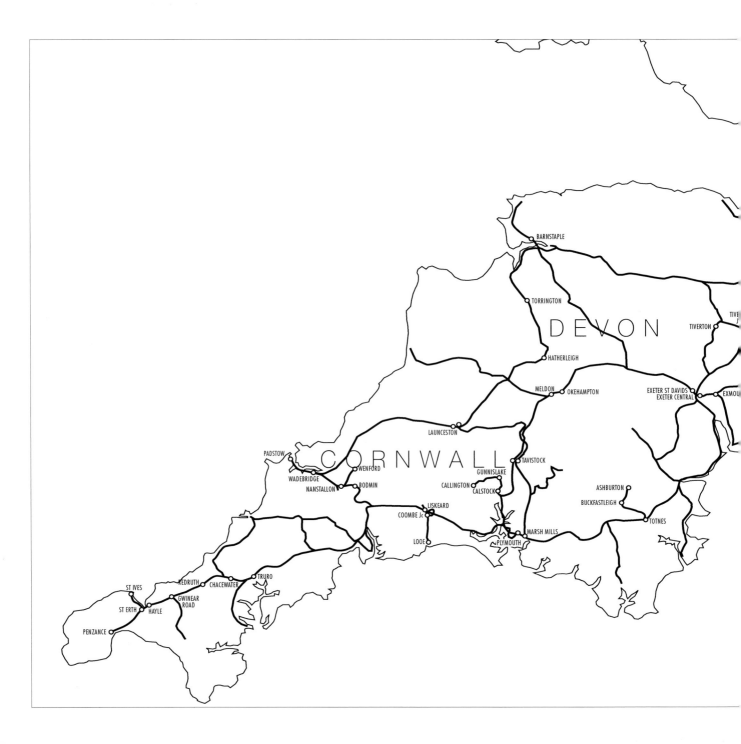

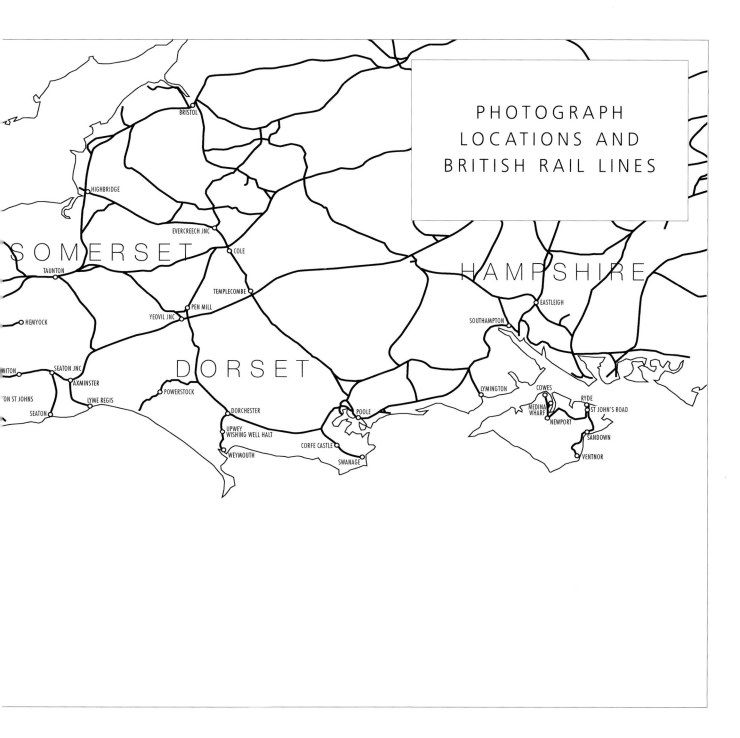

PHOTOGRAPH
LOCATIONS AND
BRITISH RAIL LINES

SOMERSET

HAMPSHIRE

DORSET

BRISTOL

HIGHBRIDGE

EVERCREECH JNC

COLE

TAUNTON

TEMPLECOMBE

PEN MILL

HEMYOCK

YEOVIL JNC

EASTLEIGH

SOUTHAMPTON

NITON

SEATON JNC

AXMINSTER

LYMINGTON

ON ST JOHNS

POWERSTOCK

LYME REGIS

COWES

SEATON

DORCHESTER

POOLE

MEDINA
WHARF

RYDE

ST JOHN'S ROAD

UPWEY
WISHING WELL HALT

NEWPORT

WEYMOUTH

CORFE CASTLE

SANDOWN

SWANAGE

VENTNOR

B.R. 6621/25

N⁰ 294

BRITISH RAILWAYS BOARD
SOUTHERN REGION

Permit .... MR. M. J. MESSENGER ....
to enter upon the British Railways Board's premises
~~between~~ ....
.... ON THE ISLE OF WIGHT ....
....

(excluding Tunnels, Viaducts, Long Bridges, Depots &
Works) for the purpose of taking photographs
from the .... 16ᵀᴴ. .... day of ...APRIL 1964....to
the.................. 15ᵀᴴ. .... day of ...APRIL 1965......
subject to the approval of the Board's Police and Officials
and to the conditions printed on the back hereof.

R. V. ACRES   D. McKENNA,
Issued by F. D. Y. FAULKNER   General Manager.

Signature of Holder.... _[signature]_

TWELVEHEADS PRESS

First published 2019 by Twelveheads Press
ISBN 978 0 906294 95 6
British Library Cataloguing-in-Publication Data.
A catalogue record for this book is available from the British Library.
Typeset in Frutiger
Printed by Short Run Press Ltd, Exeter

INTRODUCTION

My interest in railways goes back almost as far as I can remember and must have been implanted by my father. His then employer had a railway club and an early memory is of being in the cab of a very new 10001 at Willesden Junction. School, in Hertfordshire, was close to the West Coast mainline which provided lunch time entertainment. Collecting numbers soon palled for me and I decided taking photographs was better.

An early box camera provided a start but in 1958 I bought a small German camera that took eight frames on 127 film. With hindsight it was a horrible little camera and results were very poor. Fortunately it developed a fault and whilst it was being repaired I was lent an Agfa Isolette II, taking 12 frames on 120 film, 6cm square. The results were astoundingly better but I could not afford £5 for the second-hand Agfa. But it showed me the way to go and once I had started work in Truro, the family having moved to Cornwall, and had more spare cash I bought a similar Zeiss medium format folding camera. That was later superceded by a Rolleiflex twin-lens reflex.

Even in the late fifties I realised that steam was on the way out and I set out to capture what I could. I did not anticipate that much of the railway system was also to go, nor did I appreciate then that the underlying infrastructure and the working methods were much as developed by the Victorians. But in pursuing steam I captured much else.

My career took me from West Cornwall through to Devon and each move made a different part of the west country more accessible. This book then is a selection of some of my better photographs showing what I saw around the south and west of England. In the main I have avoided shed portraits of locomotives alone but endeavoured to include views that are, perhaps, a little different. It is intentionally a personal selection of photographs that I think are interesting or simply ones that I like. The trend is west to east and roughly chronological reflecting my own perambulations.

The best of the box camera photographs and one of my earliest railway photographs. W22 *Brading* at Ryde Pierhead in 1956, taken whilst visiting friends on the Isle of Wight.

The first photograph taken with my Zeiss bode well for my future photographs. 5098 *Clifford Castle* heading for Penzance with a passenger train. The location was known as Iron Bridge but now seems to be called Saveock Bridge, passing under the main road to the east of Chacewater. May 1961

(left) Steam was still common on the Cornish main line in 1962. Bringing a down passenger train in to Gwinear Road is 1008 *County of Cardigan*. To the right, running straight ahead, is the Helston branch and the vans in the sidings reflect the volume of freight traffic both on the branch and the main-line then. June 1962

(left) 1008 *County of Cardigan* leaves Highertown Tunnel, just west of Truro, with a local passenger train for Penzance. July 1962

A boy watches as 1000 *County of Middlesex* leaves Redruth with a train for Manchester. October 1962

6875 *Hindford Grange* had taken a short working from Truro to Redruth and returns with the empty stock. September 1962

Photographing the Postal train was always difficult due the late hour it ran. There was just enough light at 9pm to capture 5975 *Winslow Hall* approaching the pick-up apparatus at Liskeard while the postman waits by his hut. June 1962

A Truro regular, 6826 *Nannerth Grange*, climbs out of Truro with a passenger train for Penzance. County Hall dominates the background while the Truro breakdown train is in the foreground. June 1962

Probably the most spectacular approach to any Cornish seaside resort is that to St Ives with fine views across the bay. 4570 rounds Porthminster Point bringing the branch train in from St Erth. July 1961

4570 leaves St Ives for St Erth, crossing the rebuilt viaduct and probably ignored by most of the holidaymakers on Porthminster beach beyond. July 1961

(left) A Newquay bound train crosses Goonbell Viaduct on the Chacewater-Newquay branch, hauled by a 45xx 2-6-2T which I failed to identify. July 1961

Most of the Cornish branch lines were worked by the 45xx class of 2-6-2 tank locomotives, very capable machines. Here 5562 leaves Gwinear Road for Helston. June 1962

(left) The ex-Southern lines in Cornwall were a marked contrast to the former Great Western, with locomotives and trains of quite different character. And the North Cornwall line alongside the Camel Estuary was especially attractive. Here 31843 crosses Little Petherick Creek with a mixed train for Padstow. The trackbed and bridge are now part of the popular Camel Trail, for walkers and cyclists. April 1964

The lines into Wadebridge from the east were two single tracks, the North Cornwall line on the left and the route to Bodmin on the right, hence 34035 *Shaftesbury* appears to be on the wrong road. The Padstow portion of the Atlantic Coast Express is nearing the end its long run from Waterloo. June 1962

Heading for Padstow, O2 class 0-4-4 tank 30199 leaves Wadebridge with coaching set 24. August 1961

(opposite) 31837 has just crossed Little Petherick Bridge with a passenger train from Padstow to Okehampton. The beginnings of Padstow can be glimpsed on the far right. April 1964

The N-class 2-6-0s based at Wadebridge handled traffic on all three lines radiating from Wadebridge. Here 31836 leaves Wade-bridge with a Bodmin North to Padstow passenger working. On the right is one of the Bodmin & Wadebridge Railway buildings dating from the first half of the nineteen century. September 1962

Wadebridge was where GWR and Southern met although until dieselisation the two 'sides' operated as almost separate organisations. 1367 was allocated here for the Southern line to Wenford and 31837 arrives with an Okehampton to Padstow train. April 1964

4574 shunting empty stock at Wadebridge with, in the background, on the shed road two Beattie well-tanks and two GWR panniers that are to replace them. August 1961

The signalman leans from his box at Wadebridge East to hand over the token for 4574 and a B set going to Bodmin General. August 1961

In 1962 a limited number of Southern trains worked through to Bodmin General. By now Ivatt Class 2 tanks had replaced the O2s at Wadebridge, and 41284 pulls up the bank towards Bodmin General. March 1962

(left) The Bodmin North to Wadebridge service is worked by O2 30199 and an ex-Southern two coach set. In 1895 the building of this station destroyed most traces of the original 1834 Bodmin & Wadebridge Railway terminus and, in turn, all trace of this station has now disappeared since closure in 1967. August 1961

Ex-GWR panniers were at Wadebridge for a short time for local workings and here 4694 waits at Bodmin North with set 25 forming the Padstow train. September 1962

The climb from Dunmere Junction to Bodmin North is at about 1 in 50 and late on a March afternoon 41284 climbs the branch. March 1962

The bridge over the River Camel at Dunmere is the third structure at this location. 41275 crosses the river on its way to Bodmin North. April 1964

Bodmin Gaol provided much passenger traffic for the Bodmin & Wadebridge Railway when public hangings took place but such trade finished many years ago. Passing the gaol and a typical LSWR signal is 41284 and a train from Padstow. March 1962

In 1964 the former Bodmin & Wadebridge Railway was still very much a local line, used for school journeys and shopping trips. At Nanstallon the ladies head home with their shopping while the signalman is cadging some coal from the train crew, and the guard looks on.
April 1964

(left) One of the attractions at Wadebridge was the fleet of elderly Beattie well-tanks, maintained there to work the mineral line to Wenford Bridge. 30585, dating from 1874, prepares to leaves Boscarne Junction with the morning freight to Wenford. November 1961

I had a permit to travel in the brake van of the train so had plenty of opportunity for photography but the low sun combined with the gleaming white clay-covered surfaces at the Wenford Clay Sidings did present difficulties. November 1961

(left) The Looe branch is another picturesque branch with its origins in a mineral railway dating from 1860. A connection to the main-line was opened in 1901 and here 5531 descends the steep connection from Liskeard to the reversing point at Coombe Junction. It will continue down the line on the right to Looe. August 1961

At Looe on the last day of steam working, 5531 takes water. September 1961

By the time I reached the Callington branch for the first time Ivatt tanks had taken over services. 41323 has arrived at Callington. September 1963

(right) Common sense was a good substitute for 'health and safety' in the 1960s and the station master at Calstock gave me permission to walk over the viaduct to the Devon side of the Tamar, knowing I could do so between trains. 41315 crosses with a train to Bere Alston from Gunnislake. October 1963

A landmark in Cornish railway history was reached on 3 May 1964 when what was expected to be the last steam train ran to Penzance. A joint Plymouth Railway Circle and Railway Correspondence & Travel Society special was headed by 34002 *Salisbury* and, with my father driving, we chased it by car from Truro to Penzance. Here it crosses Hayle Viaduct. Beyond the end of the train is Hayle station with its distinctive signal box, all now demolished. May 1964

At Penzance crowds turned out to see the special and Chyandour Cliff, on the right, was packed with spectators waiting to see the return trip depart. May 1964

On the outskirts of Plymouth 4555 heads away from Laira bound for Launceston. Road improvements have destroyed this scene totally. September 1962

The Launceston branch met the South Devon main-line at Tavistock Junction, and just to the north was the first station on the branch, at Marsh Mills. 5572 departs propelling an auto-coach from Tavistock. The sidings behind, here with china clay wagons, served a tarmac and roadstone plant. March 1962

(right) Tavistock South, with its overall roof, was a busy station with a frequent service to Plymouth and through trains from Launceston. On a sunny day 6430 propels empty auto-coach W234W through the station. June 1962

5544 brings a freight from Launceston, bound for Plymouth, into Tavistock South, its guard leaning out of the brake van flag at the ready. On the left the fireman of 5568 watches as his loco fills with water. June 1962

(opposite) One of the small prairies, 4555 waits to depart Launceston for Plymouth. This location is the former Southern station, the GWR one was on the right. June 1962

A little later 4555 takes water at Tavistock South before continuing to Plymouth. At the far end of the station an auto-coach waits to move into the up platform. June 1962

The last train on the Ashburton branch was a brake-van special run by the Plymouth Railway Circle. It was hauled by 4567 and seen here at Ashburton. The line later re-opened as the Dart Valley Railway, now the South Devon Railway, but is now only able to run as far as Buckfastleigh. September 1962

Crowds were out at Buckfastleigh to see the last train. The station is clearly recognisable today as the principal station of the South Devon Railway. September 1962

The Great Western Society had acquired 1363 along with an ex-GWR coach. For a time they were kept, and occasionally run, at Totnes Quay. Seen here on an open day. 1363 normally resides at Didcot these days. October 1964

Services on the lines to Tiverton, both the Exe Valley line from Exeter to Morebath and Dulverton and the 'Tivvy Bumper' to Tiverton Junction, were operated with 14xx 0-4-2Ts.1450 is now preserved in Tiverton Museum but is here approaching Halberton Halt with auto-coach W228W. The apple trees growing alongside the track proved to be cider apples, as I quickly found when I picked an apple and eagerly bit into it. October 1964

Tiverton was an impressive station, typical of a number of GWR stations in the west country. The auto-coach worked by 1450 which is working the shuttle to Tiverton Junction waits in the down platform. October 1964

Hemyock was delightful branch, the former Culm Valley Light Railway, and due to weight restrictions was also worked by 14xx tanks. It always enjoyed much agricultural traffic and in its later years was kept open for milk traffic. 1451 is shunting milk tanks at Hemyock, and beyond the distinctive station building, a typical design of the line's engineer, Arthur Cadlick Pain, are the dairy buildings, always known at the 'milk factory'. August 1962

1451 has arrived at Hemyock from Tiverton Junction with its single coach, ex-Barry Railway W268W. These elderly coaches were retained for the branch for their gas lighting, the speeds on the branch being too slow to charge up the usual coach batteries. August 1962

In north Devon a light railway of very different character was the North Devon & Cornwall Junction Light Railway, running from Torrington to Halwill Junction. Opened as late as 1925 the line did not achieve the hopes of its promoters, although ball clay traffic was quite heavy. I was often the only passenger on its trains. 41314 has arrived at Torrington from Halwill Junction. August 1962

41314 takes water at Hatherleigh. Note the ground frame; the intermediate stations did not run to full signal boxes. The station building is now a private house. August 1962

Special trains were very much a feature of the early 1960s, British Railways being quite keen to encourage enthusiasts. The Plymouth Railway Circle special 'The Exmoor Ranger' crosses Barnstaple bridge hauled by 3205 on its way to Ilfracombe. 27 March 1965

Another special, the Locomotive Club of Great Britain's East Devon tour was hauled by 41206 and 4666. It is seen here at Tipton St Johns whilst traversing the Southern branches in East Devon. 28 February 1965

A feature of the Southern's line to Plymouth from Exeter was Meldon Viaduct carrying the line over the West Okement Valley, west of Okehampton on the fringe of Dartmoor. 31846 takes the up Atlantic Coast Express from Plymouth over this novel iron and steel viaduct, now a listed structure.

On the same date 34061 *73 Squadron* brings the Padstow portion of the up Atlantic Coast Express across Meldon Viaduct. There is now a cycleway and footpath across the viaduct. March 1964

Meldon was the source of much of the Southern Region's ballast and at this time the quarry was owned by the railway. 34007 *Wadebridge*, now preserved, brings a ballast train towards Okehampton. March 1965

(opposite) A line-up of front ends at Exmouth Junction shed. From right to left; 4610, 41275, 34106 *Lydford* and 34033 *Chard*. July 1964

A view of Exmouth Junction motive power depot, a busy shed with a wide range of locomotives based there. Classes visible include N 2-6-0, Ivatt Class 2 2-6-2T, Bullied light pacifics 4-6-2, in both streamlined and rebuilt forms and, possibly, an odd M7 0-4-4T. July 1964

Southern trains were faced with a steep climb from Exeter St Davids to Central, said to be the steepest length of main-line at 1 in 37, and steam trains needed banking. Passing over Bonhay Road 34078 is hauling the Okehampton to Surbiton car carrier and is banked by 4694 and 4692. The climbing steam engines were even more impressive at night when columns of sparks shot high into the sky. August 1964

Waiting their turn for banking duty at Exeter St Davids are 0-8-0 tanks 30955, 30956 and 30957.
August 1962

In June 1964 I moved to work in Honiton and whilst waiting at Exeter Central for my connecting train a Meldon ballast train was brought up the bank from St Davids. 80039 piloted 31837 whilst at the rear 4692 and 4694 provided assistance. It was an impressive sight and sound.
June 1964

Moving to Honiton was fortuitous as the ex-Southern line to Exeter was still worked by steam and photographic opportunities abounded. Honiton Bank was a popular location where trains climbed hard up to Honiton Tunnel. My attempt to capture a dramatic photograph was a bit too daring as the hot oil from the motion splashed me as Merchant Navy class 35013 *Blue Funnel* approached the tunnel with a down express passenger.
August 1964

BR Standard 4-6-0 76030 accelerates away from Honiton Tunnel with an up freight.
August 1964

(opposite) The up Meldon ballast train was brought to Honiton in the afternoon and continued its journey late in the evening. 34057 *Biggin Hill* pulls away from the siding under the gaze of the signalman.
August 1964

At Spilcombe, just east of Honiton Tunnel, unrebuilt Battle of Britain Class light pacific 34084 *253 Squadron* passes with an up passenger train. August 1964

In 1965 a shortage of diesel multiple units in the London area brought steam back to a number of East Devon branches. I am told that the presence of a Great Western auto-train on the Seaton branch had been 'engineered' by enthusiastic railwaymen. Looking quite at home in a Southern setting 1442 waits at Seaton for the return to Seaton Junction. March 1965

A damp day at Lyme Regis. 41320 has arrived with a single coach from Axminster. November 1963

The Lyme Regis branch briefly returned to steam in February 1965. 41307 takes the evening train from Axminster, its smokebox adorned with chalked warnings to shed staff that it was not 'self cleaning'. I had warned the driver that I would be taking a flash photograph but, in the event, he was not looking.

73001 departs Cole in a cloud of steam with a southbound train, from Bristol to Bournemouth. I was sure that the driver had opened his cylinder cocks deliberately to spoil my photograph, but without success. November 1965

The Somerset & Dorset Railway too was served solely by steam, and was reasonably accessible from East Devon. Cole, a charming station, was a popular spot with me. Standard Class 4-6-0 75072 leaves Cole with a Bournemouth to Bristol train. November 1965

Evercreech Junction was where the Highbridge branch of the S&D parted company with the main-line. 41283 leaves with a Highbridge to Templecombe train, past the rather tall signal box. November 1965

41283 waits to leave Evercreech Junction for Templecombe with its train from Highbridge. On the left 41223 has arrived from Templecombe and terminated. November 1965

Locomotive depots in country areas can be a far cry from the bustling city sheds. At Templecombe 80043, 80041, 41307 and 41296 simmer waiting their next turn of duty. November 1965

For a time the Highbridge branch was in the hands of ex-GWR 0-6-0s such as 3210 here. Highbridge S&D station was at right-angles to the Great Western main-line, immediately behind the camera.

Another interesting location was Yeovil Junction, in the background here. A special train from Waterloo is in charge of 34100 *Appledore* and 45493. Having reversed at the junction it is pulling away towards Yeovil Pen Mill where it will reverse again and head south to Weymouth on the line in the foreground. I shall see it later in Weymouth. July 1966

Yeovil was another place where Great Western and Southern met. 4569 is arriving at Yeovil Pen Mill station with a train from Taunton. May 1964

Locomotive sheds, particularly round houses, can be atmospheric places for photography. In this view at Bristol, Barrow Road 4920 is framed between 73003 and a pannier. March 1965

(opposite) Bristol, Barrow Road with GWR, LMS and BR standard locomotives visible through the sunbeams. March 1965

(opposite) A line-up of (rebuilt) Bulleid front ends at Weymouth shed; 34034 *Honiton*, 35012 *United States Lines* and 35008 *Orient Line*. April 1967

A view from the coaling stage at Weymouth, 76005 prominent. April 1967

The line from Waterloo to Weymouth was the last main line to be run by steam and became increasingly popular for steam specials, often hauled by locomotives from other parts of the country. The hillside by Upwey Wishing Well Halt provided a grand view of trains working hard on the steep bank out of Weymouth, and attracted many enthusiasts. One such special was hauled by 60024 *Kingfisher* and banked by 73114. March 1966

The special seen at Yeovil [page 66] continued to Weymouth and made the trip through Weymouth's street to the Quay. 41298 hauls the train gently through the traffic and, out of the picture, is escorted by a man with a red flag. July 1966

The Swanage branch was also a late stronghold of steam. 80146 leaves Corfe Castle for Swanage. June1964

One scene that can still be seen today, albeit rather busier. 34023 *Blackmoor Vale* brings an enthusiast special, the LCGB Dorset Coast Express, into Swanage past the engine shed and turntable. May 1967

Corfe Castle dominates the view as 80011 heads the return journey of the Dorset Coast Express. 34023 is at the rear. On the left are the narrow gauge sidings of Fayle's clay works. May 1967

One should remember that not all trains in steam days were romantic expresses. The 10.05 two-coach train from Swanage to Wareham is rather over powered with 34047 *Callington* and 80146. August 1966

I failed to visit the Bridport branch when it was worked by steam but did see this LCGB special at Powerstock, on a gloomy January day. 41320 and 41295 top and tail the train. January 1967

In the rain, another LCGB special crossing the main road at Poole, hauled by 34023 *Blackmoor Vale*, a popular engine for specials. October 1966

Southampton Central with its clock tower always looked an impressive station. 34002 *Salisbury* has arrived with a Plymouth to Brighton train. June 1964

(opposite) A visit to Eastleigh works found A1x Terrier 32678 dating from 1880 in course of restoration for display at Butlins, Minehead. It is now running on the Kent & East Sussex Railway. June 1964

Also in the works was 30837, an S15 4-6-0. It was to be withdrawn just fifteen months later and subsequently cut up. June 1964

Lymington Pier served the Isle of Wight ferry to Yarmouth, the ferry *Freshwater* can be seen on the right. 41314 was working the branch service from Brockenhurst. June 1964

I was fortunate in having friends living in Ryde, close to St Johns Road station, so visits to the Isle of Wight were quite regular in the sixties. The usual point of arrival was Ryde Pierhead where a large and busy railway terminus sat nearly half a mile out to sea. W26 stands at the water tank while W16 waits with a Ventnor bound train. June 1964

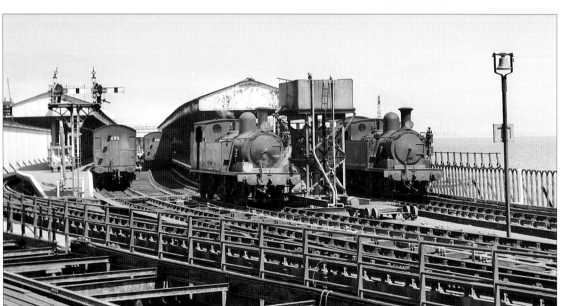

W35 approaches Ryde Esplanade at low tide with an evening train to Ventnor. June 1964

(opposite) Emerging from Ryde Tunnel with a flurry of busy steam W28 is heading for Ventnor. June 1964

W20 waits at St Johns Road whilst parcels are unloaded. The train has come from Shanklin. September 1966

St Johns Road was the location of the island's motive power depot, left, and works, right. W24 is leaving for Shanklin, the Ventnor line having been cut back to there. September 1966

The Westinghouse air-pumps with their distinctive beat were a constant feature on the island railways. W14, W30 and W18 line up photogenically with W21 on the left. August 1965

(left) At Newport the line crosses the River Medina on a low viaduct, here crossed by W14 leaving with a Cowes to Pierhead train. June 1964

W33 arrives at Newport with a train from Ryde for Cowes. June 1964

(opposite) A St Johns Road to Newport freight arrives at the latter place with W29. Some of the elderly rolling stock on the island can be glimpsed on the left. The island was a living railway museum with many of the coaches and wagons dating from pre-Grouping days. June 1964

(left) Coal and other goods were brought onto the island at the railway owned Medina Wharf, between Newport and Cowes. W30 brings the daily freight away from Medina Wharf. June 1964

Leaving Cowes with an afternoon train to Pierhead is W27. June 1964

W27 crosses Dodnor Bridge,
a mile or so north of Newport,
on the way to Cowes.
June 1964

W20 backs its stock out of Cowes station in order to run-round. August 1965

W21 waits to leave Cowes for Ryde Pierhead. June 1964

By 1966 the island railways had been reduced to a single line from Ryde to Shanklin. W20, returning to Ryde, arrives at Sandown. September 1966

W28 arrives at Ventnor, emerging from the lengthy tunnel under St Boniface Down. The signalman waits for the token. June 1964

Ventnor station was dramatically sited in a quarry high above the town. In this birds eye view W20 leaves for Ryde. August 1965

While the railway was busy the surroundings at Ventnor look distinctively rustic. W20 waits to leave.
August 1965

W28 glimpsed
from a store in the
quarry wall,
Ventnor.
June 1964

Not a very bright photograph but my very last of a British Railways (standard gauge) steam hauled train on regular duty. 34021 *Dartmoor* leaves Dorchester with a perishables train from Weymouth to Westbury. July 1967